By Sabrina Mesko

HEALING MUDRAS
Yoga for Your Hands
Random House - Original edition

POWER MUDRAS
Yoga Hand Postures for Women
Random House - Original edition

MUDRA - Gestures of POWER
DVD - Sounds True

CHAKRA MUDRAS DVD set
HAND YOGA for Vitality, Creativity and Success
HAND YOGA for Concentration, Love and Longevity

HEALING MUDRAS
Yoga for Your Hands - New Edition

HEALING MUDRAS - 3 New Editions in full color:
Healing Mudras I. ~ For Your Body, II. ~ Mind, III. ~ Soul

POWER MUDRAS
Yoga Hand Postures for Women - New Edition

MUDRA THERAPY
Hand Yoga for Pain Management and Conquering Illness

YOGA MIND
45 Meditations for Inner Peace, Prosperity and Protection

MUDRAS for ASTROLOGICAL SIGNS
Volumes I. ~ XII.
MUDRAS for ARIES, TAURUS, GEMINI, CANCER, LEO, VIRGO,
LIBRA, SCORPIO, SAGITTARIUS, CAPRICORN, AQUARIUS, PISCES
12 Book Series

LOVE MUDRAS
Hand Yoga for Two

MUDRAS AND CRYSTALS
The Alchemy of Energy Protection

THE HOLISTIC CAREGIVER
A Guidebook for at-home care in late stage of Alzheimer's and dementia

MUDRAS

for

ARIES

By Sabrina Mesko Ph.D.H.

The material contained in this book has been written for informational purposes and is not intended as a substitute for medical advice nor is it intended to diagnose, treat, cure, or prevent disease. If you have a medical issue or illness, consult a qualified physician.

A Mudra Hands™ Book
Published by Mudra Hands Publishing
Arnica Press

Copyright © 2013, 2024 Sabrina Mesko Ph.D.H.

Photography by Mara
Animal photography by Sabrina Mesko
Illustrations by Kiar Mesko
Cover photo by Mara

Printed in the United States of America

ISBN-13: 978-0615917221
ISBN-10: 0615917224

For all my Aries Friends

TABLE OF CONTENTS

THE MUDRA PRACTICE IS A
COMPLIMENTARY HEALING TECHNIQUE,
THAT OFFERS FAST AND EFFECTIVE
POSITIVE RESULTS.

MUDRAS WORK HARMONIOUSLY
WITH OTHER TRADITIONAL,
ALTERNATIVE AND COMPLEMENTARY
HEALING PROTOCOLS.

THEY HELP RESTORE DEPLETED
SUBTLE ENERGY STATES
AND OPTIMIZE THE PRACTITIONER'S
OVERALL STATE OF WELLNESS.

Mudras for ARIES

MARCH 21 - APRIL 20

BODY
Head, eyes, brain

PLANET
Mars

COLORS
Red

ELEMENT
Fire

STONES and GEMS
Diamond, Bloodstone, Fire stone

ANIMAL
Rams and Sheep

Introduction

E ver since I can remember, I have been fascinated by the never-ending view of the stars in the sky and the presence of other mysterious planets. As a child I wondered for hours about where does the Universe end and when my Father explained the possibility that time and space exist in a very different way than we imagined, my mind went wild with possibilities. I was however quite skeptical about astrology in general until one day in my early youth, a dear friend introduced me to a true Master of Vedic Astrology. He quickly and completely diminished any of my doubts about how precise certain facts can be revealed in one's Celestial map.

It was as if an invisible veil had been removed, and I was granted a peek over to the other side. The astrologer also adamantly pointed out that nothing is written in stone and one's destiny has a lot of space to navigate thru. You can make the best of the situation if you know your given parameters. My fascination and use of astrological science continues to this day and compliments and enriches my work with other observation techniques that I use when consulting.

One is born with character aspects and potential for realization of mapped-out future events, but there is always a possibility that another road may be taken. This has to do with the choices we make. Free will is given to all of us, even though often the choices we have seem to be very limited. But still, the choices are always there, forcing us to consciously participate and eventually take responsibility for our decisions, actions, and consequences.

The science of Astrology has been around for millenniums and even though some people are still doubtful, I always remind them that there is no disputing the fact, that the Moon affects the high and low tide of our Oceans - hence our bodies consisting mostly of water are affected by planetary movements in many fascinating and profound ways. Even the biggest skeptic agrees with that fact.

The Love of the Universal Power for each one of us is unconditional, everlasting and omnipresent. No matter what kind of life-journey you have, it is the very best one designed especially for you, rest assured. And when you are experiencing life's various challenges and wishing for a smooth ride instead, keep in mind that a life filled with lessons is a life fulfilling its purpose. The tests you encounter in your daily life are your opportunities. The wisdom learned is your asset, and the experiences gained are your wealth. Your Spirit's abundance is measured by the battles you fought and how you fought them. Did you help others and leave this world a better place in any way? Your true intention matters more than you know.

Each one of us has a very unique-one of a kind celestial map placed gently, but firmly and irrevocably into effect at the precise time of our birth. There are certain aspects of one's chart that reveal possible character tendencies and predisposed behavior regarding love, partnerships, maintaining one's health, pursuit of success and a way of communicating. The benefits of knowing and understanding the effects of your chart on various aspects of your life can be profound. It can help you understand and prepare ahead of time for certain circumstances that are coming your way, which increases the possibility of a better quality of life in general.

If you knew that a specific time period could be beneficial for your career, wouldn't it be good to know that ahead of your plans? If you are aware that certain aspects of your physical constitution are predisposed to a weakness or sensitivity, wouldn't it be beneficial to pay attention and prevent a possible future health ailment?

If you can foresee that a certain time will be slower for you in achieving positive results, wouldn't it be wise to use that time for preparation for a more fortuitous timing? How many times have you attempted to pursue a dream of yours that just didn't seem to want to happen? And when you were completely exhausted and disillusioned, the fortunate opportunity presented itself, except now you were tired, overwhelmed and had no energy or enthusiasm left. Having such information ahead of time would offer you the chance to save your energy during quiet, less active time, so that when your luck is more likely, you can seize the opportunity and make the most of it.

Mudras will forever fascinate me, and I have been humbled and excited how many practitioners from around the world have written to me, grateful to have these techniques and most importantly really experiencing positive effects in time of need. Therefore, it has been a natural idea for me to combine these two of my favorite topics and create a series of Mudra sets for all twelve Astrological signs.

The Mudras depicted in this book are specifically selected for the astrological sign of Aries, with intention to help you maximize your gifts and soften the challenges that your celestial map contains.

It is important to know that each astrological chart – celestial map – contains information that can be used beneficially and there are no "bad signs" or "better sings". Your chart is unique as are you. By gaining information, knowledge and understanding what the placements of the planets offer you, your path to self-knowledge is strengthened.

I hope this book will attract astrology readers as well as meditation and yoga practitioners and help you utilize the beneficial combination of both these fascinating techniques. Knowledge will help you experience the very best possible version of your life. The biggest mystery in your life is You. Discover who you are and enjoy the journey.

And remember, no matter what life presents you with, don't forget to smile and keep a happy heart. With each experience gained you are spiritually wealthier for it. And that my friend, stays with you forever. The wisdom gained is eternally imprinted in your soul.

Blessings,

Sabrina

MUDRAS

Mudras are movements involving only fingers, hands and arms. Mudras originated in ancient Egypt where they were practiced by high priests and priestesses in sacred rituals. Mudras can be found in every culture of the world. We all use Mudras in our everyday life when gesturing while communicating and when holding our hands in various intuitive positions. Mudras used in yoga practice offer great benefits and have a tremendously positive effect on our overall state of well-being. By connecting specific fingertips and your palms in various Mudra positions, you are directly affecting complex energy currents of your subtle energy body. As numerous energy currents run thru your brain centers, Mudras help stimulate specific areas for an overall state of emotional, physical and mental well-being.

INSTRUCTIONS FOR MUDRA PRACTICE

YOUR BODY POSTURE
During the Mudra practice sit in an upright position with a straight spine, with both your feet on the ground or in a cross-legged position. Comfort is essential so that you may practice undisturbed and focus on proper practice positions.

YOUR EYES
Keep your eyes closed and gently lightly lift the gaze above the horizon.

WHERE
For achieving best results of ideal Mudra practice, it is essential that you find a peaceful place, without distractions. Once your Mudra practice is established, you can practice Mudras anywhere.

WHEN

You may practice Mudras at any time. Best times for practice are first thing in the morning and at bedtime. Avoid practicing Mudras on a full stomach, and after a big meal wait for an hour before practice.

HOW LONG

Each Mudra should be practiced for at least 3 minutes at a time. Ideal practice is 3 Mudras for 3 minutes each with a follow-up short 3 minutes of complete stillness, peace and meditation or reflection.

HOW OFTEN

You may practice Mudras every day. Explore various Mudras by selecting a Mudra that fits your specific needs for any given day.

BREATH CONTROL

Proper breathing is essential for optimal Mudra practice. There are two main breathing techniques that can be used with your practice.

LONG DEEP SLOW BREATH

Slowly and deeply inhale thru your nose while relaxing and expanding the area or your solar plexus and lower stomach. Exhale thru the nose slowly, while gently contracting the stomach area and pulling your stomach in. Pace your breathing slowly and notice the immediate calming effects. This breathing technique is appropriate for relaxation, inducing calmness and peace.

BREATH OF FIRE

Inhale and exhale thru the nose at a much faster pace while practicing the same concept of expanding navel area and contracting with each exhalation. Unless otherwise noted Mudras are generally practiced with the long, deep slow breath. The breath of fire has an energizing, recharging effect on body and is to be used only when so noted.

CHAKRAS

Along our spine, starting at the base and continuing up towards the top of your head, lie subtle energy centers – vortexes – called charkas, that have a powerful effect on the overall state of your health and well-being. The practice of Mudras profoundly affects the proper function of these energy centers and magnifies their power.

Our subtle energy body is highly sensitive to outside sensory stimuli of sound, aromas, visuals and outside electric currents that constantly surround us. Frequencies that permeate specific locations may attract or bother you. Perhaps you may feel eager to stay somewhere where the energy suits you and yet feel suffocated when the environment does not agree with you. We are all sensitive to energies, but some of us feel them more than others.

A positive blend of energies with another person can create a magnet-like effect, whereas another person's negative unharmonious subtle energy field subconsciously pushes you away.

By leading healthy lives and optimizing the proper function of charkas, you empower your subtle energy bodies adding strength to your physical body, mind and spirit. Destructive behavior like addictions and abuse weaken your Auric field and "leak" your vital energy. By maintaining a healthy Aura-energy field, you can fine-tune your natural capacity for "sensing" places, situations and people that compliment your energy frequency. In a state of "clean energy" you achieve capacity for high awareness and become your own best guide.

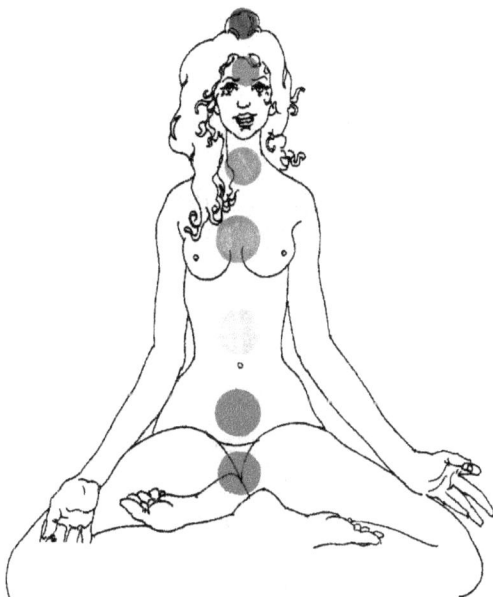

CHAKRAS IN THE BODY

Base Chakra: Foundation
Second Chakra: Sexuality
Third Chakra: Ego
Fourth Chakra: Love
Fifth Chakra: Truth
Sixth Chakra: Intuition
Seventh Chakra: Divine Wisdom

FIRST CHAKRA

LOCATION: Base of the spine
GLAND: Gonad
COLOR: Red
REPRESENTS:
Foundation, shelter, survival,
courage, inner security, vitality

SECOND CHAKRA

LOCATION: Sex organs
GLAND: Adrenal
COLOR: Orange
REPRESENTS:
Creative expression, sexuality,
procreation, family

THIRD CHAKRA

LOCATION: Solar plexus
GLAND: Pancreas
COLOR: Yellow
REPRESENTS:
Ego, intellect, emotions of fear and anger

FOURTH CHAKRA

LOCATION: Heart
GLAND: Thymus
COLOR: Green
REPRESENTS:
All matters of the heart, love,
self-love, compassion and faith

FIFTH CHAKRA
LOCATION: Throat
GLAND: Thyroid
COLOR: Blue
REPRESENTS:
Communication, truth,
higher knowledge, your voice

SIXTH CHAKRA
LOCATION: Third Eye
GLAND: Pineal
COLOR: Indigo
REPRESENTS:
Intuition, inner vision, the Third eye

SEVENTH CHAKRA
LOCATION: Top of the head - Crown
GLAND: Pituitary
COLOR: White and Violet
REPRESENTS:
The universal God consciousness,
the heavens, unity

NADIS

Your subtle energy body contains an amazing network of electric currents called Nadis. There are 72.000 energy currents that run throughout your body from toes to the top of your head as well as your fingertips. These channels of light must be clear and vibrant with life force for your optimal health and empowerment. With regular Mudra practice you can open, clear, reactivate and re-energize your energy currents.

Your Hands and Fingers

While practicing Mudras you are magnifying the effects of the Solar system on your physical, mental and spiritual body. Each finger is influenced by the following planets:

THE THUMB - MARS
THE INDEX FINGER – JUPITER
THE MIDDLE FINGER – SATURN
THE RING FINGER – THE SUN
THE LITTLE FINGER – MERCURY

MANTRA

Combining the Mudra practice with appropriate Mantras magnifies the beneficial effects of these ancient self-healing techniques.

The hard palate in your mouth has 58 energy meridian points that connect to and affect your entire body.

By singing, speaking or whispering Mantras, you touch these energy points in a specific order that is beneficial and has a harmonious and healing effect on your physical, mental and spiritual state.

The ancient science of Mantras helps you reactivate nadis, magnifies and empowers your energy field, improves your concentration and stills your mind.

About Astrology

The word Horoscope originates from a Latin word ORA – hour and SCOPOS – view. One could presume that Horoscope means "a look into your hour of birth." The precise moment of your birth determines your celestial set-up. An accurate astrological chart can reveal most detailed aspects of your life, your character, your gifts, your future possible events, challenges that await you, lucky events that are bestowed upon you, and your outlook for happy relationships, successful careers, accomplishments, health and many possible variations of life events. I say possible, because your decisions will determine the outcome.

There are 12 signs in the Zodiac and your birthday reflects the position of your Sun sign. The specific positions of other planets in your chart are calculated considering the precise moment – hour and minute and of course location of your birth. The birth time will reveal your Rising or Ascending sign, which will further determine other essential facts of your chart.

The constant transitional movements of the Planets affect each one of us differently, a time that may be difficult for some may prove supremely lucky for another and yet we are all interconnected by mutual effects of continuous planetary movements. Nothing is standing still; the changes are ongoing. On a different note, a few slow-moving planets connect us in other ways, as they keep certain generations under specific aspects and influences. We are all inseparable and in continuous motion.

There are numerous fascinating ways to use astrology and there is no doubt that the constant motion of all these powerful and majestic Planets in our Solar system affect each and every one of us differently. Astrology can be used as an additional tool to help you continue progressing on the mysterious life journey of self-discovery and self-realization.

Remember, the power of decision is yours as is the responsibility for consequences. Make peace with your doubts, pursue your dreams and relish in results.

When the outcome is less than what you expected, learn to pick yourself up and continue on, wiser with knowledge you gained, that alone being a good reason for remaining optimistic. When the outcome surpasses your expectations, well, then you will know what to do…mostly take a breath, smile, and enjoy the moment.

YOUR SUN SIGN

There are 12 signs in the Zodiac. The day of your birth determines your Sun-sign. Most often this is the extent of average person's knowledge and interest in astrology. However, the other aspects in the astrological chart are equally as important and need to be taken into consideration.

In this book your main guide is your Sun sign's dispositions, tendencies, weaknesses and gifts. Certainly, there are endless combinations of charts, and your Sun sign alone will not reveal the complete picture of your celestial map. For more detailed information and reflection about your chart, you need to know your ascending-rising sign.

YOUR ASCENDING-RISING SIGN

Your rising sign, also known as the ascendant, reflects the degree of ecliptic rising over the eastern horizon at the precise moment of your birth. It reveals the foundation of your personality. That means that even if you have the same birthday with someone else, your time of birth would create completely different aspects and influences in your chart. No two people are alike. You are one of a kind and so is everyone else. However, you may have some strong similarities and timing aspects that will be often alike. Your rising sign also reveals the basis of your chart and House placements. Your rising sign determines and is in your first house. There are 12 Houses and each depicts precise in-depth information about all aspects of your physical life, emotional make and character tendencies. It is incredibly complex and fascinating. Regarding your Mudra practice in combination with your Astrological Sign, it would be beneficial to know also your Rising sign and apply Mudras that empower your Rising sign as well. For example, if your Sun sign is ARIES, but your rising sign is Libra, it would be most beneficial to practice Mudra sets for both signs.

HOW TO USE THIS BOOK

In each book of the *Mudras for the Astrological Signs* series, you will find Mudras for different astrological signs that will help you in most important areas of your life: Health, Love, Success, and Overcoming your challenging qualities. We all have them, as we also all have gifts. This book is specific for the sign of Aries. You may change your Mudra practice daily as needed, and keep in mind, that certain habits or tendencies need a longer time to adjust, change, and improve. Be patient, kind, and loving towards yourself.

MUDRAS
for TRANSCENDING
CHALLENGES

Each one of us has a few character tendencies or weaknesses that are connected to our astrological chart. To help you transcend, overcome and redirect these challenges into your beneficial assets, you can use the Mudras in this chapter.

MUDRA for DEVELOPING MEDITATION

To sit still for a few moments is a challenge for a true Aries. You may find the thought of meditation uninteresting or uneventful. You like activity and movement and certainly most of all, you enjoy being in control. But you will be surprised how interesting, enlightening, and magical a simple short meditation can be. Your fiery power will magnify beyond measure when you make a simple effort at it. Your mind will listen to you, and you will become the pioneering leader that you desire to be. Give yourself the gift of a three-minute daily Mudra meditation practice. Try it secretly and no one has to ever know that you - a wild and hot-blooded Aries child - meditate and you actually enjoy it.

CHAKRA: All chakras
COLOR: All colors
MANTRA:
SAT NAM
(Truth is God's Name, One in Spirit)

Sit with a straight spine. With the four fingers of your right hand feel the pulse on your left wrist. Press lightly and feel the pulse in each fingertip of your right hand. Close your eyes and concentrate on the beat of your pulse. All other thoughts are gone. With each pulse mentally repeat the mantra. Enjoy the peace and stillness of your mind in meditative state.

BREATH: Long, deep and slow.

MUDRA FOR TAKING YOU OUT OF DANGER

You like dangerous situations and are never afraid to cross the line. Adventures are your hobby and trouble entertain you. Even a good argument makes you feel alive and the ones who know you best are aware that you like to win the battle. That can make you appealing and attractive, but yet when you take your daring nature a step to far, better be prepared and know how to get out of trouble as quickly as you got there. This Mudra will help you balance and calm the dangerous energies that you attract and create with your daredevil nature. A great warrior knows when to quit and retrieve, so that he may exit the battle victorious and untouched. You have that gift, but on those rare occasions when you bite off more than you can chew, protect yourself with this Mudra, and create a shield of white light all around you.

CHAKRA: 7
COLOR: Violet
MANTRA:
**GUROO GUROO WAHAY GUROO,
GUROO RAAM DAS GUROO**
(As a Servant of the Infinite I receive His Wisdom)

Sit with a straight spine. Bend your elbows to the side and bring your arms up so that your hands are at a level of your face. Curl your fingers so that your fingertips are touching the top pads of your hands. Leave the thumbs out. Hold for at least three minutes.

BREATH: Long, deep and slow.

MUDRA
FOR THIRD CHAKRA

The third chakra is where we hold on to emotions like anger and fear. Many times, when you hear the call of your warrior nature, you may get overpowered by the third energy center-chakra. Letting your fiery nature overwhelm you and take over is not necessary. Fire works best when contained and controlled and it is one of your life's lessons to learn to tame your fire. It is your house-your body that you reside in, so don't let the fire burn the house down. Give it some air and redirect that valuable energy into other areas of your being and life. This Mudra will help you spread your life force through all the chakras and prevent it from sitting in one place. Balance and tame your fire and the world will be at your feet.

CHAKRA: 3

COLOR: Yellow

MANTRA:
SAT NAM
(Truth is God's Name, One in Spirit)

Sit with a straight back. Bend your elbows and lift your hands up, elbows parallel to the ground. The palms are open facing forward, all fingers together except for the thumbs. Thumbs are pointing to the ears, lightly touching your face in front of ears. Hold and keep the elbows nice and high for at least three minutes.

BREATH: Short, fast breath of fire from the navel.

MUDRAS

for HEALTH

and BEAUTY

Each astrological sign rules certain areas of your body. The Mudras in this chapter will help you strengthen your physical weaknesses while maintaining a healthy body, and a beautiful, vibrant appearance.

MUDRA for Transcending ANGER and Preventing HEADACHE

Your sign tends to be prone to head or face injuries, headache, and high fever. It is essential for your well-being, that you are familiar with this Mudra.

Instead of letting the anger take over and create a headache, practice this Mudra for three minutes and let the negative energy disappear. It will tame your fiery temper under control and help you preserve your health and a cool head so that you may continue to be the "great idea person" that you are born to be.

CHAKRA: All chakras

COLOR: All colors

MANTRA:
GOD AND I, I AND GOD ARE ONE

Sit with a straight spine. Lift your hands to the level of your eyebrows. Make fists with the palms facing outward and keep the thumbs stretched pointing towards each other. Press the point between your eyes and nose at the beginning of your eyebrow. Keep your eyes lightly open and direct the gaze gently towards the tip of your nose. Hold for at least three minutes.

BREATH: Long, deep and slow.

MUDRA for
Emotional BALANCE

This Mudra will help you keep balanced with your emotions which is essential for your health. Don't let your life's situations overwhelm your nervous system. Relaxation should become part of your daily routine and when you are ready to give yourself that gift, your inspirational nature will reach new levels of realization. Be a true example of a great leader that you were born to be. No emotions can sway your boat. You are calm and in harmony with the universe.

CHAKRA: All chakras

COLOR: All colors

MANTRA:
SAT NAM
(Truth is God's Name, One in Spirit)

Before you practice this Mudra, drink a glass of room temperature water to balance your system. Sit with a straight spine. Place both hands with palms open under your armpits. Close your eyes, inhale and give yourself a big hug and lift the shoulders toward the ears for a few moments and then lower your shoulders, exhale, relax and open your eyes. Repeat at an easy pace for three minutes.

BREATH: Long, deep and slow.

MUDRA FOR
CALMING YOUR MIND

Yes, you know how getting all worked up and excited isn't good for your health or a happy disposition. So when you feel tempted to explode and show your temperament, remind yourself that it will only make you feel better temporarily and that after a while you will look and feel exhausted. Because you are very expressive when displeased, everyone will see how you feel. That may not be great when you want to mesmerize someone with your charm which you have plenty of. One of great assets you can use is a calm and centered mind. That way, your power will magnify and incapacitate your opponent in an instant. But most of all, you will protect your health and preserve your youthful and glowing appearance.

CHAKRA: 3, 4, 6

COLOR: Yellow, green, indigo

MANTRA:
OM
(God in His Absolute State)

Sit with a straight spine. Cross your arms in front of your chest, elbows are bend and at a ninety-degree angle. Arms are parallel to the ground. Place the right palm on top of the left arm and the top of the left hand under the right arm. All fingers are together and straight. Hold and keep the elbows nice and high for all three minutes of the practice.

BREATH: Long, deep and slow.

MUDRAS
for LOVE

The Mudras in this chapter will help you understand your love temperament, your expectations, your longings and how to attract the optimal love partner into your life. It is most beneficial to know how others perceive you in the matters of the heart. It will also help you understand your partner and their astrologically influenced love map.

MUDRA TO
OPEN YOUR HEART

You love conquering your chosen target and will just about always do it successfully. Your hot sexual nature will take over and the object of your desire will be at your feet sooner rather than later. But you also need a lot of stimulation and unless your lover knows how to keep you guessing and chasing, you will quickly become bored. That may bring you into the habit of always chasing after someone new. You will avoid a deeper involvement and will leave before the romance has a chance to grow. But only when you allow your love to develop from the purely sexual fiery conquest into a full-blown affair of the heart, will you finally experience true happiness. You will be magically transformed and mesmerized and will learn to love deeply from your heart. You need to let go, open your heart, and let yourself experience the difference, the bond and mutual dance of love and sex. At the moment of realization you will transform, evolve and become very loyal to your chosen love. Happiness on a new and deeper level will emerge.

CHAKRA: 4

COLOR: Green

MANTRA:
SAT NAM
(Truth is God's Name, One in Spirit)

Sit with a straight spine. Lift your hands up in front of your heart and create a cup, palms facing up. All fingers are spread apart. The palms and fingers are not touching. Keep the fingers stretched as antennas of energy and visualize your heart area opening. Practice for three minutes.

BREATH: Long, deep and slow.

MUDRA FOR
SIXTH CHAKRA - TRUTH

Your charm, sensuality, love of danger, and adventure in your love life will have its price. To juggle all the potential activity and mesmerized conquests, you need to be and are quite clever with words, which means undoubtedly many times the truth will be "adjusted." The truth will be truth no more. This habit may hurt you when the time comes, and you get out of conquest mode and really fall in love. Instead of a tendency to serve yourself, you must respect and consider the heart of your love partner.

As uncomfortable as it may seem and feel, strive to develop the habit of being truthful with your chosen one. You will be loved for who you are, all imperfections included. Telling the truth will set you free and help you truly relax at last. This newly found habit will greatly help you with your own insecure tendency to fell jealous. Remember, be your best and in return the best will come to you tenfold.

CHAKRA: 6

COLOR: Indigo

MANTRA:
EK ONG KAR
(One creator, God is One)

Sit with a straight spine. Bend your elbows and lift your arms up so that the elbows are parallel to the ground. Palms are facing out and all fingers are together. Hold for at least three minutes. Concentrate on your Third Eye.

BREATH: Long, deep and slow.

MUDRA OF TWO HEARTS

Being in love means you are in love with someone, and a very important fact is: there are two of you in the relationship. No one knows exactly what goes on in a relationship, except the two that are in it. In love you are passionate, magical, irresistible, but also bossy and impulsive. That may be a real test for your lover. Remember to consider your lover's opinion, ask about their feelings and consult with them before assuming you are on the same page. That will spare you much conflict, help you avoid an argument and replace it with harmony and love.

As an exercise before making a hasty decision, just for a moment consider how your lover would feel about your plan of action. Your intuitive answer will be immediate and clear. This approach with the same final result will make them love and adore you even more-if that is at all possible, and you will be pleased with yourself that on top of the great passion you possess, you also have great tact.

CHAKRA: 4

COLOR: Green

MANTRA:
SAT NAM
(Truth is God's Name, One in Spirit)

Sit with a straight spine. Connect the index and the thumb fingers forming a circle. Extend all other fingers, keeping them spread out. Lift your arms up in front of your heart. Palms are facing outward, and hands are crossed over each other, left in front of right. Hook the small fingers together. All the fingers are extended. Hold for three minutes.

BREATH: Long, deep and slow.

MUDRAS
for SUCCESS

The Mudras in this chapter will offer you tools to present yourself to the world in your optimal light. Often one is confused in which direction to turn or where their strength lies. Mudras will help you focus and remember your essential creative desires; help you gain self-confidence and inner security to recognize your desired and destined path. If you know what you want, and your purpose is harmonious for the better good of all, your success is within reach.

MUDRA
FOR GUIDANCE

You are courageous and bold, driven and decisive. A great pioneer and inventor of new revolutionary projects and endeavors. You also possess great intuitive perception. In order to really take the full advantage of all these wonderful talents, you will magnify them by learning how to really listen to your inner voice of wisdom. Be still for a moment, so you can hear your guiding voice that is bubbling with new inventive ideas never heard of, seen or experienced. When you connect with your inner guide, nothing will stop you and things will happen quickly, explosively and magically. Rely on your inner wizard and watch your ideas come to life.

CHAKRA: 7

COLOR: White

Sit with a straight spine. Place your hands together in front of your chest. Little fingers are pressed together to form a cup. Palms are facing towards the sky. Leave a very small opening between the sides of the little fingers. Gently focus your eyes on the tip of your nose towards the palms. Have a clear question. Hold for three minutes, relax, be calm and wait for a clear answer.

BREATH: Long, deep and slow into your palms.

MUDRA FOR PATIENCE

You possess great drive, know how to fearlessly take the initiative and have a youthful excitement about your endeavors. That means that very often, after you've planted your revolutionary ideas, you expect the fruits to ripen overnight. Well, that is impossible. Some things need maturing and time for growth. This is the opportunity for you to practice patience. All in due time, every flower needs its time, every fruit needs nourishment and light. Provide that for your seed and practice patience. Before you know it, just after you realize there is no need to be in a tremendous hurry, your fruits will ripen.

CHAKRA: 6, 7

COLOR: Indigo, white

MANTRA:
EK ONG KAR SAT GURU PRASAAD
(One creator, Illuminated by God's Grace)

Sit with a straight spine. Make circles with the tips of your middle fingers and thumbs. Keep the rest of the fingers straight. Your upper arms are parallel to the floor and elbows are out to the sides. Your hands are at the level of your ears. Fingers are pointing towards the sky and palms are facing front. Hold for three minutes, breathe and keep the elbows nice and high.

BREATH: Long, deep and slow.

MUDRA for EFFICIENCY

There are times when you are overcome with fiery and exciting new ideas or projects. It seems that you begin them under impossible circumstances, and against all odds. Yet they take off, and you as well as everyone else can see you are onto something big. This is when you need to pay special attention. A weakness of yours is that you quickly lose interest and before a project is completed you are ready to move on and conquer the next impossible thing. Here are a few choices: either you surround yourself with an amazing team of people who are going to finish the revolutionary idea that you started, or you learn to be persistent and complete your work yourself. In either case you will need to be on top of your game and very efficient. This way, no mountaintop is unreachable, nothing is unattainable, and success is yours.

CHAKRA: 4, 6

COLOR: Green, indigo

MANTRA:
ATMA PARMATHA GURU HARI
(Soul, Supreme Soul, the Teacher
in His Supreme Power and Wisdom)

Sit with a straight spine. Bend your elbows to the side and raise your hands to the level of your heart. Palms are facing your chest, a few inches away from your body. Your hands overlap and the palm of the right hand is placed over the back of the left hand. All the fingers are extended, the thumb tips are pointing towards each other. Hold the hands and forearms parallel to the ground. Practice for at least three minutes.

BREATH: Long, deep and slow.

ABOUT THE AUTHOR

SABRINA MESKO Ph.D.H. is an International and Los Angeles Times bestselling author of the timeless classic *Healing Mudras - Yoga for your Hands* translated into fourteen languages. She authored over twenty books on Mudras, Mudra Therapy, Mudras and Astrology, Holistic Caregiving, Spirituality and Meditation techniques.

Sabrina holds a Bachelors Degree in Sensory Approaches to Healing, a Masters in Holistic Science, a Doctorate in Ancient and Modern Approaches to Healing, and a Ph.D.H in Healtheoloyy from the American Institute of Holistic Theology. She is board certified from the American Alternative medical Association and American Holistic Health Association.

She has been featured in media outlets such as The Los Angeles Times, CNBC News, Cosmopolitan, the cover of London Times Lifestyle, The Discovery Channel documentary on Hands, W magazine, First for Women, Health, Web-MD, Daily News, Focus, Yoga Journal, Australian Women's weekly, Blend, Daily Breeze, New Age, the Roseanne Show and various international live television programs. Her articles have been published in world-wide publications.

She hosted her own weekly TV show educating about health, well-being and complementary medicine. She is an executive member of the World Yoga Council and has led numerous international Yoga Therapy educational programs. She directed and produced her interactive double DVD titled *Chakra Mudras* - a Visionary awards finalist.

Sabrina also created award winning international Spa and Wellness Centers and is a motivational keynote conference speaker addressing large audiences all over the world.

She is the founder of Arnica Press, a boutique Book Publishing House. Her mission is to discover, mentor, nurture and publish unique authors with a meaningful message, that may otherwise not have an opportunity to be heard. She is the founder of world's only online Mudra Teacher and Mudra Therapy Education, Certification and Mentorship program, with her certified therapists spreading these ancient teachings in over 28 countries around the world.

www.SabrinaMesko.com